JESUS AND BUDDHA TALK:

ABOUT DESIRE, SUFFERING, AND HAPPINESS

PHUC LUU 福刘

POSSIBILITIES PRESS

JESUS AND BUDDHA TALK

PHUC LUU 福刘

979-8-9916143-4-4 ISBN Hardcover
979-8-9916143-5-1 ISBN Paperback
979-8-9916143-6-8 ISBN Ebook
979-8-9916143-7-5 Audio Book

Library of Congress Control Number: 2025908805
Printed in the United States of America
First Edition

Book design Houston Creative Space
Cover image by Freepik
Author photograph by Paula Nguyen Luu

POSSIBILITIES
Press

Praise for Jesus and Buddha Talk

"Dr. Phuc Luu has imagined a wise and beautiful conversation that portrays communion between brothers, reverence for each other's paths and perspectives, and a commitment to practicing breathing in the Spirit—the breath of life—so they may directly experience the divine unity humanity needs. This work is just what a polarized world needs right now: an inspiration to remember how to "love all our neighbors as ourselves" and to rediscover how Great Love resolves desire and suffering into lasting joy."

— **William Thiele**, PhD,
author of *The Gate of Heaven*
is Everywhere and *Monks in the World:*
Seeking God in a Frantic Culture

"Jesus and Buddha Talk: About Desire, Suffering, and Happiness is a rare and refreshing invitation into true, soul-stirring conversation. In these pages, Phuc Luu imagines what might happen if Jesus and Buddha sat down together—not to debate, but to listen, share, and explore the deepest human questions with humility and curiosity. This isn't a theological showdown, but a jazz-like dialogue full of hospitality, wisdom, and the beauty that rises from the overlap and shadows of their words. What Phuc has created is not a prescription, but a practice—an imaginative space to walk with these teachings and let them marinate. As the book so beautifully reminds us: 'There is something deeper and greater waiting to emerge—to be enlightened, to be resurrected.'"

— **Travis Reed**,
founder and filmmaker,
The Work of the People

"*Jesus and Buddha Talk*, and in their dialogue, we are invited to be present with them in the beauty and grace of the exchange that Phuc Luu helps us to imagine. As an artist, Luu chisels away what religious history has layered upon these ancient wisdom teachers. As theologian, he helps us see the simple truths of love and healing that are invaluable for our lives today. Luu's masterful book offers a new experience of two simple humans, Siddhartha and Yesua, guiding us to live more deeply human lives ourselves."

— **Jon Singletary**, PhD,
professor,
Diana R. Garland School of Social Work,
Baylor University,
author of *Leadership by the Number:
Using the Enneagram to Strengthen
Educational Leadership*

"Phuc Luu writes, 'If familiarity breeds contempt, I wish for us to become alienated from these two personalities as much as possible so that we could learn to appreciate them again.' In the book that follows, he invites us to meet Siddhartha and Yeshua anew and experience their wisdom, depth, and playfulness. It's a gift, in these times, to be invited into a place of respectful listening and transformative encounter. Luu has achieved something remarkable here: a book of Buddhist and Christian conversation that shines with new insight."

— **The Rev. Dr. Jeremy Rutledge**
Senior Minister,
Circular Congregational Church,
Charleston, SC

To my parents, Lễ and Thủ Tầm Lửu.
Even though they might not understand my path,
they provided a way.

contents

INTRODUCTION

When I first started this project, it seemed the Buddha and the Christ could offer very little to each other in agreement. As religious icons, venerated by millions of followers, each has been subjected to thousands of years of history, interpretation, dogma, and religion. Even though these ways of reading religious history have opened understanding of these two, it has also separated them, making them seem more distinct than alike.

With many sects of Buddhism come many ways of interpreting and thereby practicing the philosophy. In the West, this has taken on a particular problem of cultural appropriation. Many white U.S. Americans have adopted this philosophy and made it their own, albeit often using the cultural dress and symbolism of the East. This is of course understandable, since each sect of Buddhism is tied culturally to a particular region in South and Southeast Asia.

The same is true with Christianity. The reason for the many versions of the New Testament is the many interpretations of that work. As many denominations there are, there is a different way to read the Bible. The movement that was once called "The Way" has splintered into myriad, varying roads, and it is difficult to know how to interpret Jesus' words outside the teachings of these churches and denominations. As Christianity spreads throughout the world, one can no longer speak of it as a single, monolithic religion, but of "Christianities." However, if we strip the religions down to the historical figures, as Prince Siddhārtha Gautama and Jesus of Nazareth, both being Eastern figures, we can see that they share similar concerns and approaches to life. And it is through this lens that we can hear them speak more clearly.

During the 6th or 5th century BCE, Siddhārtha Gautama was reacting to the Vedic religion in South Asia. What we currently describe as Hinduism was not a monolithic religion at that time, but one filled with much philosophical richness and varying traditions. A common thread was the belief in the cyclical nature of life. The cosmos was governed by *saṃsāra*, the circle of birth, life, death, and rebirth. The only hope for *moksha*, or liberation from this kind of existence, was in fulfilling one's *dharma*, or duty. Living the life of a prince, Siddhārtha was sheltered from the pain of life until he encountered what is known as the "four sights": old age, sickness, death, and the ascetic life. From these experiences, he sought to diagnose the true cause of suffering to be truly liberated from this life of constant struggle. In pursuing this path, one achieved enlightenment or true liberation, called *nibbāna* in the Pali language or *nirvana* in Sanskrit. In a paradox, by breaking free from his *dharma*, Siddhārtha was able to truly pursue his *dharma*.

Similarly, Jesus' views were a response to Second Temple Judaism. These were the teachings of various sects of Judaism that made up the cultural milieux of his time. One of these groups, the Pharisees, established places of education called synagogues in many towns in ancient Palestine. There they taught the Torah, or "Law of Moses," and the various schools of interpreting the law. Even though many Jews could observe the teachings and the men were trained, like Jesus, to be Rabbis or teachers of the Law, there were others who felt ostracized by their communities. These people were the sick, crippled, poor, demonized (those we would consider having psychological diseases), and those with occupations that did not allow them to be Torah-observant Jews, such as shepherding and butchery. Because of strict laws regarding ritual purity, people who were stained with blood and even women who were menstruating were shunned from religious activities.

Since the Deuteronomic Code can be summarized by "You are blessed because you are obedient," then many took the corollary to be true, "You are cursed because you are disobedient." Hence, people lived on the margins because of the stigma that they were somehow "sinners" because of their lot in life. Jesus saw that this marginalization exasperated the problem of sin, suffering, and evil in the world. His remedy was to be with those who hurt so that their wounds could be healed, and in this healing the cycle of sin could stop. His teachings and preachings on the "Kingdom of God" were to show that these people had a place in the world and that this reign was upon them if they continued the work of restoration in each other.

If these concepts seem quite different from the standard conception of Jesus and first century Judaism portrayed by the majority of Christianity, then it is because for centuries we have read the New Testament through western lenses rather than the perspective and context of a Near Eastern society.

Ever since I read Thích Nhất Hạnh's *Going Home: Jesus and*

Buddha as Brothers and *Living Buddha, Living Christ*, I was left with the impression that there were too few books for the public that engaged insights from these two great traditions. However, within the academic discipline of religious studies, there is a wealth of resources that bring these and other religious figures together in conversation. The student can learn much about these traditions and the ways in which they interpret the meaning of life, our relationship with the universe, and how we should live. But what if I put them in actual conversation with each other to elaborate on topics that were important in their lives, and what if the reader can be free from the confines of formal academic language and hear them speak as if friends and brothers? When placed side by side, it is easy to see how the two great figures might have much to say about desire, suffering, and happiness, and that conversation might be something that we wish to eavesdrop on. We can be curious as to where the conversation might lead and gain valuable insights. We can then be a pilgrim with them on their journey to discover what made their teachings valuable for so many centuries.

For the ease of writing, I will refer to the Buddha as Siddhārtha Gautama. The title "the Buddha" or Awaken One was not an honorific that he used in his lifetime, but others bestowed on him after his death.

Similarly, I use Yēšūa for Jesus of Nazareth. This is the Aramaic version of his name, even though Latinized. The name means "to heal or to save," and writing it this way re-establishes a foreignness that too often we, in the West, forget. The title, "the Christ," is a Greek version of the Jewish designation, "the Messiah." Hebrew kings and sometimes foreign emperors, such as Cyrus the Great, were given this honorific. Jesus never used this title for himself but allowed others to refer to him as such. Instead, he often referred to himself as *bar 'anash* (Aramaic), or "Son of Humanity"—a title drawn from Jewish apocalyptic literature. Though it might seem humble or nonchalant, in its original context it carried a sense of cosmic weight and divine mystery, pointing toward a figure who stood at the threshold of judgment, transformation, and divine authority. This very ambiguity became its strength, both grounded in humanity and bearing a tinge of transcendence. Nevertheless, the title does not hold the same weight to the modern reader and therefore is lost in the chasm of time.

If familiarity breeds contempt, I wish for us to become alienated from these two personalities as much as possible so that we could learn to appreciate them again. This is not in disrespect, but to help us imagine the two speaking to each other not as icons and deities of their respective religions, but as two people seeking to listen, understand, and share about their views. In the Greek philosophical tradition, the word "dialogue" is used to express a type of logic, a "dialectic" or "speaking through." It was through speaking with a conversation partner, or interlocutor, that Socrates revealed what was true and what was not. This is what we call the "Socratic method," and it is invaluable in teaching and learning. My thought was that in this dialogue there might be something more valuable that could be brought forth than if we relegated them to their respective camps and spoke about their approaches separately.

In our present culture, especially in the West, having respectful dialogue has fallen into hard times. Most conversations seem to be speaking across one another, rather than seeing something in each other that can be a valuable insight. This is especially true when we come to topics such as politics or religion. The opposite of dialogue is dictatorship. When dictating, only one person speaks, and the other person serves to scribe or carry out their words. It is a one-sided relationship. Conversely, in dialogue, at least two people interact to obtain truth, something that transcends either's voice. In listening to these two people speak, if we are patient, we might realize the very human struggles in each of these conversation partners. If we find the humanity in them, we might just find the humanity in ourselves.

Lastly, even though this is a work of philosophy and theology, it is also one of fiction. The glossary of terms and citations of other resources are there to provide context, but to take this as pure dogma would be to misread its intent. I have drawn from the texts of Buddhism and Christianity, but I've also taken imaginative liberties—not to distort, but to illuminate. No special revelations, no hidden insights—only the creative work of listening for what might be said if two of the world's great spiritual teachers simply sat down together and spoke. What emerges is not certainty, but curiosity. Not conclusions, but companionship. And perhaps, if we're lucky, a glimpse of something true between them—and within us.

Ultimately, this book is a work of joy. Written on the path, on the way, to my own fulfillment.

Phuc Luu
Houston, Texas
Easter 2025

Desire

The air was fragrant and spring-like. Siddhārtha Gautama climbed a hill overlooking an orchard. Butterflies fluttered about, pollinating the blossoms of fruit trees. The sound of a brook cascading over rocks mingled with the distant galloping of horses. Oxen bathed in the water as dragonflies hovered above them. The grass, lush and verdant, rustled in the cool breeze.

From a basket, Siddhārtha set out two clay cups and a teapot. He poured a fragrant blend of chrysanthemum and jasmine into the cups and waited for his companion to arrive.

He could now see Yēšūa ben Yosef ascending the slope, his face glowing with a brilliant tan. Their skin tones were similar. Each wore the robes of his own culture — Siddhārtha draped in saffron, his garments crafted from three intricately woven pieces of cloth, while Yēšūa's attire was a simple one-piece chitōn in earthy browns and deep blues. On his feet were well-worn sandals, whereas Siddhārtha's feet were bare. Yet both sets of feet carried the stories of countless miles traveled.

The aroma of the tea drifted to Yēšūa's nostrils as he raised the clay cup. He blew gently across the surface to cool it before taking a long sip. The taste was delicate and crisp. Here, there was no time — only the present. And the present was the best time to speak of all that weighed upon the heart and mind.

"It's such a pleasant day to meet. The breeze is a perfect coolness on the skin. The sun radiates upon your face, my brother," Siddhārtha started to speak.

"Yes, this day welcomes us. I'm humbled by your presence, my prince," Yēšūa replied with a smile.

Siddhārtha laughed. "Ha! Please, I abandoned that veneration long ago, when I renounced a life of ceaseless pleasures and delights. I left Lumbini to seek the true nature of a life hidden behind all those desires. Do I call you the Christ?"

"We are brothers here," Yēšūa replied. "Even my original disciples did not know what to make of that designation. During my time, many messiahs came and went. All that I am cannot be contained in a single word — just as I suspect you are more than your title of Buddha, the Awakened One."

"Yes, people squabble over titles and status but fail to do what is important. They reject being who they truly are. That is the quandary of life. Too often, we do not seek what is essential — happiness, love, joy — but add so much to ourselves that we can no longer see what lies beneath.

At the same time, all that we truly need is already present with us. We do not need so much to seek happiness, but rather to awaken to its presence. Everything else is sleep.

To believe that happiness is in an object is to sleep.

To believe that happiness is in a person is to sleep.

To believe that happiness is in a career or a job is to sleep.

To believe that happiness is found anywhere but in happiness itself is to sleep.

Do I speak correctly?" Siddhārtha inquired.

"That is very true. It is a type of restless sleep.

I did not need cathedrals, nor thousands of varying beliefs, nor rituals of veneration. All I asked was that my followers love each other just as I love them. Too often, we make the simple complex. I'm sure it was the same for you," Yēšūa replied.

"Yes, I did not wish for statues nor temples. Truly, I did not ask for anything. But these things are trappings created by culture. They are not prohibited when they serve as symbols that help the follower reach something beyond themselves. Such was the Bodhi Tree — the place of enlightenment. My students, to this day, make a pilgrimage to the sacred fig tree, hoping to find enlightenment for themselves. But symbols and icons fail when they no longer reach deeply inside," Siddhārtha agreed.

"Why do you think people fall for the thing itself, rather than what the thing is helping us to achieve?" Yēšūa asked.

Siddhārtha replied, "It is easier to pour one's hopes and dreams into a representation of belief than to embody that belief in one's life. We would rather talk about the bread, where we bought the bread, and what ingredients are in the bread, rather than eat the bread."

Yēšūa added, "Is it not necessary to understand what we are practicing? There were many people in my day who spoke without a deep realization of what they were speaking about. Rabbis spoke about the law, but did not understand the essence of the law — which is a deep and singular love for God and this world."

"Absolutely. But in practice, we understand, and as we understand, we practice," Siddhārtha replied. "At some point, a blacksmith must strike the hot iron with the hammer. The steel will then tell the smith how to make the next strike.

Too often, there is too much that gets in the way of even picking up the hammer. We argue about which hammer to use, whether it is the right color, or if the fire is hot enough. All of this is not unimportant, but if it gets in the way of doing what we need to do, then we are left with nothing."

Yēšūa concurred and added, "If worship is declaring the worth of something, then it is best to do that in our acts of love toward others. It is through the extension of ourselves that we show what true worship is.

It is as one of our prophets said, 'God has told you, O human, what is good, and what does the LORD require of you, but to do justice, and to love kindness, and to walk humbly with your God?'"

Siddhārtha continued, "If people stayed on this path, then they would certainly enjoy goodness. Peace would flow into them."

"If goodness is the goal of every human path, then why do you think people choose otherwise?" Yēšūa inquired, though he had an idea of the answer.

Siddhārtha took another sip of his tea, breathed deeply, and answered, "That is the problem: desire, longing, the ceaseless wanting."

Yēšūa clarified, "That was your enlightenment — the problem you diagnosed in our life."

Siddhārtha continued, "Yes. *Taṇhā*, in my Pali language. It is a thirst, a longing that ignites the fire."

"But that is beautiful. It's the flame. It's the light," Yēšūa said.

"But it burned me up from inside. It was my poison. It led to greed, to anger, to delusion," Siddhārtha responded.

Yēšūa prompted, "Please say more. I feel it is something that has not fully ceased in you."

Siddhārtha clarified, "It is not something that goes out forever. I extinguish it daily, at every moment, or else it becomes an unending appetite. There are not enough luxuries — gold, delicious food, beautiful women — to quench that thirst. And when those things cannot be had, anger grows inside.

It is the feeling that somehow I did not receive my just due of all the world's riches and offerings. This is the delusion — that somehow it is never enough. It is difficult to see through it all, difficult to lift the veil."

Yēšūa took a long sip of his tea and added, "But anger can be a wonderful thing, leading to justice. It can motivate us to do good, to say enough is enough.

When religious leaders took advantage of the poor to line their pockets at the Jerusalem Temple, I was furious and cast them out. My father's house was not a concession stand for the greedy or a monopoly for opportunists."

Siddhārtha concurred, "Yes, you speak truth. Perhaps you are more disciplined than I am when it comes to controlling your emotions. Too often, our anger is not about the injustices of the world, but about how we have been slighted.

There is the darker side of anger that finds its way into bitterness and violence when it cannot get what it wants. This is the great deception, isn't it? That we can trust what we perceive.

The world is what the Vedic tradition of my land calls *māyā*, or illusion. We think it's an oasis, but it turns out to be a mirage. It deceives us into believing that is what we want, but it's only empty sand."

A ladybug landed on Yēšūa's arm. Picking it up with one finger, he brought it to a nearby rock. It crawled for a moment and then fluttered away.

Yēšūa's elaborated, "I can see how we are easily fooled. Too often, when people are deceived, it is because they want to be deceived. They want to see something that is not there.

Seeing is not believing. But there must be some sight, some vision of another reality. Even my disciple, Thomas, had to see me to know I was real."

"What more is there to see? Except to close your eyes, and then you can be completely satisfied with what you have. You can quench your desire, or at least extinguish the flame for the moment," Siddhārtha said, tilting back his head to demonstrate.

Yēšūa nodded. "Yes, I feel that too. There are many temptations. I could have had it all — to be a prince, like you.

In the Judean desert, where I fasted for forty days, I encountered my own demons. I was tempted to turn stones into bread to satiate my painful hunger.

I was tested to prove God's reality to the world by making a showy promise of salvation — that if I jumped from the highest peak, God would save me, and I would prove myself worthy to all.

Lastly, I was offered dominion over the kingdoms of the world and their wealth, if I would only bow down and worship the devil.

It would have been easy for me to become a king, to conquer a nation. I had followers who were willing to rise in insurrection against the occupying empire.

But none of this would have quenched my thirst. It was all empty power."

"Then how did you resist? How did you avoid the trap?" Siddhārtha asked.

Yēšūa took a deep breath. "I delved into the root of my desires. My hunger was for something that would truly satisfy. My thirst was for something eternal. Even though I was fasting in the desert, my heart feasted on the words of God. They were my bread and water. I sought fulfillment through feeling the hunger."

Siddhārtha prompted, "So you found your way in your desire, not away from it."

Yēšūa explained, "Desire exists as a result of human nature. We crave more than what satiates the body. We seek to explore the extent of our power, the limits of our abilities.

Most people are afraid of what their hearts want, and therefore they choose only what they can get. The tangible is always easier than the intangible.

To want to be well is not only about being free from sickness. It is about wholeness, connection, meaning."

Siddhārtha continued, "Yes, that is a tricky position. That is why attachment, avoidance, and ignorance entangle us so easily — a briar patch.

We want what we want, and if we pretend not to, it only means we want it even more."

"Did you not face these same temptations?" Yēšūa prompted.

Siddhārtha answered, "Yes. Māra was my Evil One, my tempter.

This occurred when I was leaving my estate to become a Bodhisattva, a seeker of enlightenment. Māra met me at the gate and offered to make me a Chakravarti — a monarch over the entire earth. Imagine that!" Siddhārtha shook his head in amazement.

Not only prince over my Shakya clan, but emperor over the world. But I denounced this and continued my journey.

Later, while fasting severely, I encountered Māra again, who told me that if I rose and ate, I would live and do good works. But I refused and told Māra that I would rather die in battle than live a defeated life.

The last temptation was under the Bodhi Tree, where Māra sent legions of demons to attack me. But their arrows turned into fragrant flowers. Māra then sent his daughters — Lust, Folly, and Envy — to entice me to return, but their treats and temptations did not move me. I stood my ground."

"That too seems difficult to defeat. How did you strengthen your resolve?" Yēšūa asked.

"A magician's act is no longer magical when you know how it is done.

The mind must be quieted. It must focus not on what captivates it, but on listening to itself — its inner being.

The breath.

At last, this is all we possess: the ability to breathe and to listen to this breath.

This is our being.

If *nibbāna* is the quenching of the flame of desire, then the breath is the only way we can blow it out," Siddhārtha said, puffing gently with his mouth to illustrate.

Yēšūa added, "I call this the Spirit. It is the breath of life. It is what makes the soul. Furthermore, it is what animates us. The divine name, *HaShem*, is said to be this breath."

Placing his palm over his heart, he continued, "Even in the Vedas, the tradition that I grew up in, the divine Spirit, Brahman, is said to be breath."

"All things are connected." Yēšūa raised his hand, stirred it through the air, and brought it together with his other hand.

"Ah. Let us take a deep breath of this Spirit," Siddhārtha said happily. He inhaled deeply, filling his belly as a baby breathes, and exhaled with a gentle sound.

Yēšūa mimicked him and concurred, "Yes, it feels good to breathe deeply — taking in what we require and releasing all that we do not need into the world."

"Brother, could you please pour me some more tea?" Siddhārtha asked with a smile.

"Certainly, my friend." Yēšūa pondered aloud as he lifted the clay pot and slowly poured the tea into the empty cup. "It seems that your desire was to eliminate desire, which was the cause of suffering.

Perhaps it is not desire that is the problem, but too many competing desires."

The golden liquid in Siddhārtha's cup swirled, appearing like a glistening galaxy.

Siddhārtha thanked him and prompted, "Please continue."

"I desired to have many things, including a family like you had. But my life's journey was to help heal and free those who suffered from the cycle of oppression and hurt. Ultimately, I did not abandon family, but instead found those whom I would call sister and brother.

I desired to fulfill a call for something greater than what I had imagined for myself — and it returned tenfold, a hundredfold.

I found what I truly wanted: to do the will of another, to accomplish something far beyond myself. In doing so, I satiated my true longings and measured my true abilities."

Siddhārtha pressed, "How did desire not turn into ambition, into greed and folly?

The resolve of people is not strong. Their hearts are fickle. They want one thing one day and another thing the next. They are tempted by too many distractions and therefore never find what they are truly after."

"Yes, you understand clearly the heart of the problem — and it is the heart itself.

We are pulled and prodded by desire, but this desire can be a good thing. It can lead to children, to the welfare of our families and neighbors, to striving for a better way of life. But it can also be our downfall.

According to the Talmud in our tradition, there was a time when the rabbis of Israel prayed to God to remove the *yetzer hara* — what is called the 'evil inclination.' God granted them this wish, and all they desired was to pray and devote themselves to the study of Torah.

However, they soon found themselves starving, neglecting their wives, and watching their households fall apart.

Our desires can go either way.

The heart is like an arrow. It needs to be directed. If it is not, it misses the mark."

"Ah," Siddhārtha said with understanding. "You call this 'sin' in your language."

Yĕšūa answered, "Yes, but it's *not* essentially moral. It is not about right and wrong. No one misses the mark on purpose. They are either led astray or do not know any better. Willfully doing so speaks of maliciousness — and most people want to do well for themselves, if not for others."

"Then how do you help people down the right path, to the correct road, toward the way?" Siddhārtha asked.

"One must first allow the heart to heal. The first desire should be to heal desire. The first step to being well is to want to be well."

"Don't all people want to be made well?" Siddhārtha inquired.

"Not necessarily. Most people are content to be where they are. Even though we may say we want better, to actually be better is another thing.

It is the plight of who we are. Change involves giving up something of ourselves and embracing something else."

Siddhārtha concurred, "Very true."

"That's my line. Ha!" Yĕšūa laughed.

"But isn't that the problem? We think we know who we are

and therefore do not want what is given to us. This belief is a deception," Siddhārtha asserted.

"Say more, my friend."

"We are constantly changing, from birth to death. At every moment, there is an opportunity to let go and to accept.

If we hold on to who we think we are, there is no opportunity for growth, no opportunity to see who we can become — and therefore, who we truly are.

We would rather spend our energy resisting change than embracing it."

"Do you mean sometimes people resist being healed?"

"We've both seen this in our ministries. Some people would rather continue to be in constant battle rather than assume peace. Some people would rather wallow in brokenness than be well. They want peace and healing, yet fear to take it."

"Yes. A healed heart freely receives and freely gives. Otherwise, it will continue to hurt itself and others."

Siddhārtha inquired, "How is the heart — the metaphorical place of desire — healed? How can we truly want to be made well?"

"We must learn to love in the way that is in right relation to ourselves, others, and the world."

Siddhārtha clarified, "You are talking about being in harmony."

"Yes, that is right. We say this in the *Shema Yisrael*, our daily prayer: 'God is *echad*. God is one.'"

"Harmony is a middle path. The tension that tunes the string. It is the way between sensual indulgence and self-mortification, between self-satisfaction and self-denial.

This, then, is the problem of the self, the ego," Siddhārtha responded.

Yēšūa urged, "Say more about the self."

"There is nothing to say. There is no permanent, independent self. The word *anattā* describes the absence of this kind of self.

We are all in a state of flux. There is no mine, no me, no self. If we realize this point, then desire easily vanishes," Siddhārtha continued.

"So it appears that avoiding both self-satisfaction and self-denial is easier if there is no self to contend with," Yĕšūa replied.

"Correct," Siddhārtha confirmed.

Yĕšūa added, "Yes, denial of self is essential. But also, the restoration of the self is equally important.

I like to think of it as emptying the self to fulfill the self. My life was one of pouring out my divine self to take on the form of a human self.

And for people, they must take this road in the opposite direction — to empty out their human selves to have union with the divine.

At least, this was the path I was leading them toward."

"That is quite a feat of liberation. Do you think that assuming this glorified state would purge them of their wrong desires?" Siddhārtha asked.

"This was the way that I sought to make for them."

"Then what kept them from walking this path and completing the journey? Why does the world not look like the kingdom of heaven that you wish for them to be citizens of?" Siddhārtha asked.

"When they no longer sought healing, but rather sought acquittal from their wrongdoings, this was where things went astray.

Instead of seeing the world as a place of restoration, they made it a place where hurt continued to fester.

Forgiveness was handed out instead of caring for the wounds that were inflicted.

People preferred easy grace over acts of compassion. They wanted absolution rather than loving their neighbor."

Siddhārtha asked, "So did they not seek healing, or did they seek it in the wrong ways?"

"Both.

To be cured of sickness, one must first admit one is sick.

But people often deny their sickness even while seeking self-medication and treatment in all sorts of ways.

As you know, people pursue many remedies to soothe a broken heart. But none of these ways truly heal."

Siddhārtha asserted, "It is the same with my followers.

Incense and prayers were not what I wanted, but mindfulness — following the Eightfold Path toward enlightenment.

Many of my people were guilty of starting wars and committing atrocities against others and against the earth.

I never wanted Buddhists, and perhaps you never wanted Christians either.

The goal was for people to awaken to the realities of the world."

"At first, my disciples were all Palestinian Jews," Yēšūa said. "And I wanted to provide a vision of what the world could be.

I was pursuing a new sense of family, community, and peace — not a new religion.

It was not that I did not want others to experience this great hope, but the idea was not to build more beliefs — it was to enter into another reality.

It appears that neither of us got what we wanted."

Siddhārtha concurred, "Such is the chasm between what we intended to do and what eventually happened.

I once told the story of the water snake to my students. One man sought to capture a water snake, but he grasped it by its tail, and it turned around to bite him.

Another man used a stick to pin the snake down and grasped it by the head. He was able to take control of it.

Proper grasp of any teaching is important.

People who are not careful misinterpret us with their words and actions. They not only cause harm to others, but also to themselves.

However, those who are meticulous enough to grasp our teachings correctly receive what they set out to capture."

"There are many careless interpreters of our teachings, are there not?" Yēšūa said. "They haphazardly take metaphors and turn them into facts, and facts into metaphors.

Rather than grasping the truth to find freedom, they are bitten in their efforts to prove themselves right."

"But let us not dwell on how people twist our words. Let us dwell on what is.

That is why desire is at the root of the problem for me.

For you, it seems that it is the direction — it provides the path to a goal."

Yēšūa pondered, "Yes. The goal says much about the desire."

Siddhārtha returned, "But does it not speak to who we are — our human nature? Are we something, or are we nothing?

If we are something, then what is it that we are?

Our nature determines our pursuits, does it not?"

Yēšūa suggested, "We are human, and we are beings.

We were made to pursue our highest good.

We seek to survive, and we also seek more than our most basic needs. And we need help to get there.

Given our finite natures, we cannot achieve our good alone. We need each other.

And I know this as well: that you are my brother," Yēšūa said tenderly.

Siddhārtha added, "And you are mine.

So there is indeed something that I possess. However transitory my state, I do not exist to myself alone."

"We can both hold these things lightly and hold them tightly. Both—and," Yēšūa responded.

"I can appreciate that."

JESUS AND BUDDHA TALK

SUFFERING

Siddhārtha gazed out toward the landscape, taking in its beauty. It was eternity in an instant, and he sought to feel its texture with all his being. There was nothing like it, and there would never be again.

"Shall we speak next about suffering?" Siddhārtha inquired.

"You pick such light subjects, my friend," Yēšūa chuckled with a large grin.

He held one hand over his heart and the other outstretched and open, signaling him to continue.

"Is it because suffering cannot touch us where we are now?" Siddhārtha asked.

"But a person can have everything and still suffer," Yēšūa replied.

"That is very true," Yēšūa said with a smile.

Siddhārtha returned with a similar smile. "You seem not to be bothered by the desire that is in you. You are very passionate."

"We are stirred by the things we love. This desire helps us grow into the people we are meant to become. Babies desire to suckle, and people desire companionship. Unmet desires contort our hearts into something ugly, such as deceit and violence. Fulfilled desires lead us to long for continued growth. At the same time, desire not tethered to the flourishing of other relationships also leads to damage and decay."

Siddhārtha added, "Our word *duḥkha* means unease. It is the result of desire."

"You are correct. Desire can bring much suffering. But it can also bring much joy. Just as a shadow is the result of light, suffering can accompany desire. But don't we need the light? God has put eternity in our hearts, and that longing leads us down a path back to where we need to be."

Siddhārtha asked, "Where is that, might I ask? Is that heaven?"

"If heaven is union, return, wholeness, then yes. But I'm not talking about an after-life existence. I'm talking about the possibility of now—an eternal now."

"Yes, to be present is an eternal way of being. Our minds too often wander—we live in the past with regrets, resentments, and grief, or in the future with anxiety, worry, and uncertainty. But neither truly exists—there is no past and no future. There is only now, and that is a place most people do not know how to dwell in," Siddhārtha concurred.

Yēšūa asked, "Does that bring suffering?"

"Yes, for many. We suffer because we cannot have what we think we want, and even when we receive it, we want more. The millionaire wants to be the billionaire. Romantic love fades, and people start looking at others to satisfy what they think is missing. There is never enough prestige or fame or power. Not having it leads to suffering. But also, not being in the present moment, where everything is, is also suffering."

"How about the suffering of disease, starvation, and death? Ceasing those cravings does not lessen this kind of suffering," inquired Yēšūa.

"When I left my palace for a tour of my kingdom, I came upon four sights that lingered—they brought me to the reality of the suffering of this world. My father, King Suddhodana and leader of the Shakya, told me to ride out to send a decree to all the land so they would make the streets look beautiful and smell wonderful. It was a massive infrastructure project of our time. I was on my royal chariot, surrounded by attendants and followers. And me, I was twirling a flower as if there was no care in this world."

Siddhārtha sighed and continued, "On the way to the capital city, Kapilavastu, I spotted an old man. I asked Channa, my charioteer, why this man's hair was white and why his clothes were but rags. He explained the man was old in years. I was only twenty-nine at that time, younger than you when you started your ministry. Much of my life was sheltered behind the palace walls. So, I did not have knowledge of great age and its decay to the body. Channa explained to me that all people eventually turned out this way.

Further into my trip, I encountered a sick man, who lay on the side of the road. He was diseased and abandoned. Rushing over, I tried to alleviate his pain, but there was nothing I could do. Channa informed me that this was the fate of many. It was to my surprise because I had access to many healers and sages. Long-term sickness was alien to me.

Finally, the chariot was stalled by a funeral procession. The mourners were carrying a dead man. Channa told me, to my dismay, that this was the final fate of all mortal beings—to die. It was the inevitable end to all life. I knew this in theory, but never saw it with my own eyes."

Yēšūa asked, "What then was the fourth sight?"

"It was the ascetic, the one who wished to escape this life, to embrace something more than this continual cycle of birth, death, and rebirth, what is called saṃsāra. It was a spiral that many wished to escape but found themselves stuck, with no hope in this world and only a glimmer of possibility in the next.

Instead, I wanted to know the root cause of our suffering," Siddhārtha answered.

Yēšūa asked, "How did cessation of your desire also stop the real suffering?"

"Those before me believed in *moksha*, the liberation from desire, through walking the path of *dharma*—right action without attachment. But I wanted the cycle to stop now, and not in a reincarnated life to come. Therefore, there must be a path to achieve this, there must be a right way of living that would provide the course to alleviate the ache of desire.

When I was a prince, my father made me take archery lessons. Imagine if an arrow would stray off course and hit someone nearby, what would the first response be? Is it to ask why the arrow hit the bystander? Is it to ask what the essence of the arrow is? Is it to know who made the arrow or what it is made of? Of course not. The first response is to overcome the pain, to relieve the suffering."

Yēšūa added, "Some people see their suffering as unbearable and seek to end their suffering by taking their own lives. They think this will bring them peace."

Siddhārtha agreed, "The problem is that it adds to the suffering of those they leave behind. If we think our lives are so difficult and our grief so great that it is not worth living, then we are most likely alone in our suffering. But seldom are we the only ones affected by our hurt."

Yēšūa clarified, "When one person hurts, all hurt. Pain too often makes us feel as if we are the only ones experiencing it. Pain has a way of deceiving us into believing we are the only one suffering. Even though our pain is personal, it is never isolated. If suffering can be shared, it can be softened. In my life, my suffering was never mine alone."

Siddhārtha continued, "Yes, it is too often a product of our perception that we see ourselves as being singular, a world unto ourselves."

Yēšūa added, "And people seem to think they know many things about death that they do not. Our friend, Socrates, understood this point well and said that the one thing he knew was that he did not know much about anything, and this was especially true regarding death."

Siddhārtha reflected, "When he was convicted and sentenced to death, many grieved his passing. Even though Socrates took the poison hemlock willingly, as he was following through with his civic commitment to the law, this did not make his people better or bring about a more just society. Plato and other disciples took up his cause and continued his work."

"Too many people think that the death of another would put an end to another's suffering, or restore justice, or obtain what they really want. That is a mistake also," Yēšūa said.

Siddhārtha stated, "The only way to end suffering is to deal with the source, desire."

Yēšūa continued, "Your journey showed you the inevitable side of the human condition, and you sought the remedy. To wonder why we suffer is ultimately fruitless. That is extremely wise."

Siddhārtha asked, "And how did you deal with suffering? It appears that your life was filled with it as well. The people who you were with were diseased and distressed. They were poor and sick and even despised. Some were like the Dalit of my culture, the broken, the untouchables."

"Yes, they were the sick and sinned-against. I had the power to heal their wounds, but greater than that, I walked beside them. My attempt was to show them that God was present in their lives even when they experienced profound absence. Most religious people offered them the hope of God's forgiveness and blessings, like a carrot on a stick, but instead ostracized them and exacerbated their hurt. They said that it had to be earned through the sacrifice of their money and time. In some cases, as with those who were sick and had birth defects, they were accused of being cursed because of some sin of their own or their parents. Instead, I tried to teach them with the ministry of presence, to sit with each other in their hurt, desperation, and despair. This was the way to heal their wounds.

Instead of calling them 'sinners,' I offered forgiveness of sins, freely. In that way, they could believe that they did not do anything deserving of God's punishment or retribution. Even though I received much criticism for this, and was even called a blasphemer, I would rather forgive them of a so-called 'sin' than let them languish in anger, fear, and guilt for something that they did not deserve. I would rather receive condemnation for heresy than allow people not to live a life free from the thought of God's fictitious wrath. So when I told them, 'Your sins are forgiven,' it was a gift, not an absolution. They didn't need to be sorry because they had done no wrong against me or God in their poverty, sickness, or despair. These words were meant to liberate—because no one else was offering forgiveness to them."

"What about those who truly harmed the innocent?" Siddhārtha asked.

"I offered them a chance to be healed—to turn from wrong

and choose what was right. Often, they were the ones most in need of mending. But pride and self-righteousness made it difficult for them to receive it. Yet for those who needed me most, healing came—because they could receive it."

Siddhārtha nodded. "So you became compassionate in the real sense of the word. You suffered with your people."

Yēšūa added, "You know of compassion since another moniker was given to you as the Compassionate Buddha."

Siddhārtha smiled and said wryly, "I blush at that, my dear brother. But compassion also implies passion and suffering. It is a difficult road. You also suffered as much as your people. It seems that living a life of passion can also be a life of suffering."

Yēšūa explained, "My longing and my sorrow were not lived alone, but through and in my people. I sometimes suffered with them. I sometimes suffered because of them. But that is what love is about, isn't it?"

Siddhārtha invited, "Tell me more about how love and suffering relate."

"Love is bound to suffering. Without love there can be no suffering. And suffering can be changed into hope by love," Yēšūa elaborated. "Love changed me, transformed me, broke my heart and filled it up. Anything touched by love cannot help but be changed by it. The more love we have, the more suffering, but also the more we become open to the world."

"How is love transformative?" Siddhārtha urged.

"When a mother loves a child, love changes her. When a person loves another, love changes them. They cannot stay the same. This is the true meaning of suffering. It is not only about pain. It is about the possibility of being different. As we grow, we might experience it as painful, but that is only our sense of it. We are often married to the idea of our former selves; we don't know how to grieve what was lost and hold on to that notion of the past as much as possible. However, does a butterfly think about its life as a caterpillar? Does a person miss their existence in the womb?"

Siddhārtha responded, "But many people are broken by love. They grieve, and their grief sometimes turns to bitterness, hard-heartedness, and resentment. They regret that they opened themselves up to it to begin with.

Once, there was a woman, the wife of a wealthy man, named Savatthi, who came to me grief-struck because of the death of her only child. She was in such denial that she went from house to house searching for a remedy for her deceased boy. People thought she had gone mad, but I saw the heart of her pain. However, so that she could see it herself, I told her she could bring back her child if she could find a white mustard seed from a house that had never seen death. She followed my direction, only to see that every family had suffered the anguish of losing someone. Only then could she bury her son."

Yēšūa responded, "People who can grieve this deeply are able to testify to the truth that they loved so profoundly that it shattered them. Yes, they can become resentful and lash out. They can become bitter and enraged. This only reveals how tender they are. Only that kind of heart needs much protection. But the only way to heal a wound is to expose it, disinfect it, and allow it to mend.

Trust me, I've been wounded many times by the insults and brutality of others, but the only way to not be broken by love is to forgive. It is to give others the love and respect that one needs for oneself. It is to turn heartache into empathy for hurt. Sometimes the perpetrators are those who are the most damaged of all because in hurting others, they continue to hurt themselves.

The easiest way is to become the source of love itself. When we are this, then love, even when painful, also heals."

Siddhārtha commented, "To grieve well and forgive well are not easy tasks, but it is the path to living well.

You are truly the Bodhisattva, the one who delays the attainment of achieving *nibbāna* so that they could help the suffering and those in need. You could see the other side of the wall to paradise, yet you remained behind to serve."

Yēšūa replied with a gentle smile, "Now, I am the one to be humbled by your veneration. But I never sought to be on the other side of the wall, as you describe it. My goal in living this life was to help others attain what was meant for them, true fulfillment through connection to all things. I was to mend the broken-hearted and bind up their wounds."

Siddhārtha continued, "Yes, this is what we both sought to achieve, to live rightly with all beings, however great and small. All things are us, and we are all things. All things change and dissolve into everything else. We are all changing. This is the truth of *anicca*, or impermanence. Those who deny this truth and attempt to cling to what they perceive as unchanging truly suffer. Holding on to youth is suffering. Holding on to the past is suffering. Holding on to this life is suffering."

Yēšūa nodded thoughtfully and replied, "There is profound truth in this. Even if suffering cannot be relieved, what we make of our suffering can change its meaning."

Intrigued by this perspective, Siddhārtha encouraged further, "Please say more."

Yēšūa continued, "Before I was betrayed, I told my disciples to pray for me, and I went out alone into the olive trees in anguish because of what would soon happen. It was so distressing that drops of blood dripped from my brow as sweat, and tears streamed down my face. I asked that this path would be removed from me and that I would not have to drink from this bitter cup.

But I resolved not to do what I wanted, but to do what my father wished, which was to continue to be faithful to my work."

However, what I wanted and what God wanted both turned out to be the same. My deepest desire was the restoration of humanity and helping people realize the greatness of the Kingdom to come. The outcome was not what I wanted, but this could not be averted. The greater the task, the greater the resistance to achieving it.

After my death, I was resurrected, and my disciples were given the strength to continue my work.

Love triumphed over evil and sin. Life was victorious over death.

We can do something with the suffering we all receive. When our hearts ache, they can speak words that can help us shape the trajectory of our lives. My pain, my heartache, even my crucifixion could be made into something meaningful. It could be turned into a message that the divine identifies with all those unjustly crucified in this world.

All those who are imprisoned without cause.

All those people who were victims of slavery and execution.

All those oppressed by religious and political powers.

My death, as a victim of Roman politics and religious persecution, speaks to a world where people suffer in similar ways."

Siddhārtha concluded, "You took your pain and turned it into something beautiful, to send a message about the suffering of others. It seems that your death has been grossly misinterpreted, as a way to save people from eternal punishment, rather than a story of how God suffered with all the crucified."

Yēšūa added, "That is the transformation of suffering, turning suffering into passion."

"Yes. That's the crux of it. No pun intended," Siddhārtha humored.

"Ha!"

"Too soon?"

Yēšūa continued, "Those who are passionate suffer much. But those who suffer can also let their passions consume them, snakes eating their own tails. It's a never-ending cycle. Poets, artists, and philosophers easily fall victim to this if they are not careful."

Siddhārtha elaborated, "Yes, our word is *dukkha*. It is a deep dissatisfaction, uneasiness, dis-ease, if you will. Suffering plagues us all."

"My brother, you know suffering as much as I do. Your life was not easy either. You left your wife and son to become an ascetic to find the cause of suffering. Did you achieve what you were searching for?" Yēšūa asked.

"I lived a long life, and one mainly of peace. What I tried to do was transform my own life into one that achieved harmony with others. However, before setting out to do this, I became an austere ascetic and shaved my long black hair. I exchanged my princely garments for the orange robes of a monk. All I owned was given away for a beggar's bowl. This was in service of seeking the root cause of suffering."

Yēšūa inquired, "So you entered suffering to find its cause? You were both the physician and patient?"

"Yes. You can say that.

I sought out the greatest spiritual teachers of the day and subjected my life to one of severe austerity. My frame was skeletal thin. My skin burned in the midday sun, and my body froze in the cold of night. I slept on a bed of thorns to subdue the flesh, and even spent nights in cemeteries. I was near death until a young girl offered me a bowl of rice. At this, I realized that this kind of extreme living did not lead to enlightenment, but more suffering.

This was when those few disciples who were following me saw my weakness and abandoned me."

"I can thoroughly relate!" Yĕšūa said with a smile.

Siddhārtha could not hold back a chuckle and continued, "It was at Bodh Gaya, I sat and meditated throughout that night beneath a pipal tree."

"That was where the demon attacked," Yĕšūa added.

"Is it not the truth that before every breakthrough there is terrible struggle? Something in us seeks to be born anew. And it is immensely painful," Siddhārtha reflected.

"Yes, I used the same image of birth, but few understood it. Tell me more," urged Yĕšūa.

"Under the Bodhi tree, I slipped into deep meditation and saw that my suffering was due to my greed, hatred, and delusion, as I mentioned before. This was my awakening. To extinguish the flame, I had to put an end to desire and its poisonous roots.

At first, I was hesitant to share what I received, but then realized how many still had dust in their eyes and were blinded to see the path ahead. So, at Isipatana, I met with those disciples who had previously left me and delivered my first sermon at Deer Park. It was an auspicious moment, and that started my ministry for almost fifty years. To first teach the middle way, then the Four Noble Truths of suffering, which are the problem of suffering, its cause, the prescription, and the remedy. Eventually, this led to the Eightfold Path."

"That is quite a journey you have made to relieve suffering and obtain peace," Yĕšūa remarked.

"The journey takes us to places we can never consider, to places we cannot conceive. It brings peace to our suffering when we reach our destination," Siddhārtha replied.

Yĕšūa inquired, "Can we say that is where happiness is?"

Happiness

Siddhārtha pondered for a moment and asserted, "People say money is not the key to happiness."

"Very true," Yēšūa replied.

"...but if you had enough money," Siddhārtha said with a smirk, "couldn't you just have a key made?"

"Ha! You jest! That's delightful."

"I thought you would like it. In your first sermon, did you not speak of happiness?" Siddhārtha then asked.

"Yes. I taught my disciples that happy were the poor, both the ones in spirit and the ones in poverty. Theirs will be the Kingdom of Heaven.

Happy are those who are grieving, for they will be comforted.

Happy are those whom others find insignificant, for they will inherit the earth.

Happy are those who hunger and thirst for justice, for they will be fulfilled.

Happy are the merciful; they will be shown mercy likewise.

Happy are the pure in heart, for they will see God.

Happy are the peacemakers, for they will be called children of God.

Happy are those who are persecuted for seeking justice, for theirs is the Kingdom of Heaven."

"So even in poverty they could be happy?" Siddhārtha inquired.

"And even in riches, they could still be happy. As you know, poverty is not a blessing, nor are riches a blessing. Happiness in itself is the blessing because it is the most difficult to attain."

Siddhārtha asked, "What then is happiness?"

Yēšūa pondered for a second, "Happiness is in the connection we have with others, the world, and the core of being. True happiness goes beyond what *happens* to us externally—the good fortunes, the circumstances, the luck we might have."

Siddhārtha answered, "One of my disciples would say that there is no path to happiness, but happiness is the path. Do you think this is so?"

"Yes, I couldn't agree more. This is the route that all people seek. A philosopher once said that we do all things seemingly in pursuit of happiness. But you are saying, 'Why not simply start there?'"

"Precisely. If we become happy rather than seeking to be happy, then the path is clearer." Siddhārtha smiled.

"Speaking about path, let us take a walk," Yēšūa suggested.

Siddhārtha got up from his cross-legged position and the two walked across the grass into a grove of cherry blossoms. The wind plucked the flowers into the air, and the petals swam around the two as if a school of fish. The smell was of lilac, magnolia, almond, and a hint of vanilla. The sun cast an orange blanket across the green expanse, the shadows of the two following them on the grass. Yēšūa's hands held each other behind his back, while Siddhārtha spoke with his.

Siddhārtha continued, "Why did you then choose poverty if happiness is elusive in both cases?"

"Who said I was not rich? I was fulfilled more so than the wealthiest kings in the world. I saw abundance everywhere, even in the Judean desert. The misconception was that I was somehow a poor beggar. I observed the richness of all life and how the problems in my world were caused by people who could not perceive this very notion. This was why people hoard their wealth and do not share. They see the world as a pie. If someone gets a piece, then they don't.

Rather, the world is a banquet table to be enjoyed by all. This is the reason so many people live impoverished lives; they are always wanting more. They constantly live in scarcity, in the lack, and perceive absence of what they think they need and want. The Kingdom was a reign of abundance for all. This is why so many of my parables and teachings were about wages, and treasure, and money. There are plenty of resources to go around. There is enough of God to go around.

But this was the most threatening message of all. The political powers disliked it because they wanted to control the resources—who gets to have what. The religious people hated this because they wanted to control people's relationship with God—who owns the right doctrines, who owns the right beliefs.

I entered a life of teaching and service because so many of my people were poor and sick, demonized and disenfranchised. They lived on the fringes of our society and needed to see that God would meet them there as well. Those who were wealthy also sought me out. They deeply felt God's absence, even though God was not far from them either.

There was once a very wealthy man who asked how he could live well, to have, as we called it, 'eternal life.' He had many possessions and much money, but still, he did not know how to live in deep abundance. I told him to sell all he had, give it to the poor, and follow me," Yēšūa explained.

Siddhārtha asked, "Did he do what you asked of him?"

"He walked away, saddened by the choice he had to make. It seemed he had tied his happiness to his possessions... and that was why he could not live well."

Siddhārtha reflected for a bit and replied, "I thoroughly know the truth of this. Riches are not the problem. It is the value we give to them that diminishes our lives. I once thought the ascetic life was the answer. I thought that abandoning everything, even to the point of starvation, was the key to happiness. It was not. It was in my work with others, my community, my *sangha*, that brought me to true fulfillment. What is a teacher without their students?

Besides, there are many people in poverty who have much money, and there are many people who feel wealthy with very little."

"I entirely agree. I depended on my community for the food I received, a place to rest my head, even learning from them," Yēšūa concurred.

"Yes, I am deeply thankful for what I received."

"Deep gratitude is the key to happiness," Yēšūa agreed and paused. "You see what I did there?"

"Ha! You are a wise and funny one, my friend," Siddhārtha responded, "The Risible One!"

"Touché! You make my heart full!"

Siddhārtha placed a hand on his chest and said, "I am thankful for our friendship, for this day, for the tea, for the air we breathe, for being."

Yēšūa agreed, "It is the easiest task, to be grateful. Yet so many take all this for granted. It is as if they seek to be unhappy when happiness is in each and every moment."

Siddhārtha thought for a moment and replied, "A man told me once, 'I want happiness.' And I responded, 'First remove "I," that's ego, then remove "want," that's desire. See now you are left with only "happiness."'"

Yēšūa replied, "Happiness then is the state that you are in. It is where you are now. That is the place."

Siddhārtha added, "Babies are born happy. We grow up and learn how to be unhappy. We are unhappy with ourselves, our lives, our spouse, our family, our friends, our work, our possessions. It is endless unhappiness."

Yēšūa countered, "But babies also cry. They get upset when they don't have what they need—mother's milk, a caring and warm embrace."

Siddhārtha responded, "But good parents know this and let them suckle and give them love.

If we see our interdependence—that all things are interrelated—then the happiness of another person is our own happiness. When we see the clouds, we see the paper, as one of my disciples would say. When we see ourselves in the other, we can be happy."

Yēšūa prompted, "Please say more about this interdependence."

Siddhārtha explained, "It's about how all things relate and cannot be separated. Causes and effects need not happen one after the other. An effect of one thing can be the cause of another, and the opposite is true. We can look at the clouds and see a sheet of paper. The clouds give way to rain. The rain waters the trees. The tree yields the wood. The wood is used to make the paper. If we see all things as being in us and us in all things, the wanting and the need dissolve. We possess all.

We can drink of this truth deeply."

Yēšūa agreed, "Yes, people do not learn to drink from the source of life, especially when it is readily available to them. They instead quench their thirst with what does not bring fulfillment. Over and over, they drink from tainted waters, waters that make them feel full and fulfilled but leave them empty. They make their lips more parched and become more dissatisfied."

Siddhārtha explained, "This is why I teach my disciples the Eightfold Path that starts with the three trainings: virtue, mind, and wisdom. Virtue being right speech, right action, right livelihood. Mind being right effort, right mindfulness, right concentration. Wisdom being right view and right intention.

We start with the Five Precepts, where we abstain from killing living beings, stealing, sexual misconduct, lying, and intoxication. It is a difficult path, but I have found that this leads to a happy life. It is our code that upholds our *sangha*. It also upholds the universe." Siddhārtha lifted his hands, opened to the sky, as if cradling the universe and releasing it at the same time.

Yēšūa pondered, "It seems that your teachings helped you and your disciples to relate to others and the world around you. You are attempting to be in constant harmony."

"The most important part is to set ourselves on the path of right thinking. Who we are is the result of what we have thought," Siddhārtha replied.

Yēšūa explored, "It seems our thoughts can pave the path."

"Our thoughts form the foundation of who we are. We are made up of our thoughts. If one speaks or acts with an evil thought, pain follows, as the wheel follows the foot of the ox that pulls the wagon.

If one speaks or acts with a pure thought, happiness follows, like a shadow that never leaves," Siddhārtha explained. He paused and then asked, "You have similar teachings as well, do you not?"

"Certainly, but many find them difficult since they are not only about our actions but, like you, consider our intentions. They are of the heart.

Some have chosen to interpret my words harshly and have punished their flesh to subdue their desires. They live austere lives, depriving themselves of any pleasures. But this is not my wish for them. I do not wish upon anyone more pain, or suffering, or even sacrifice. Yet, the path is deeper still."

"So, some of your followers are ascetics also—nuns, monks, hermits, and the like, are they not?" Siddhārtha questioned.

"Yes, God meets everyone where they are—to their ability, they are given. But if they choose to pursue something greater, they will be led there as well. I go only where their hearts will take me. Sometimes it is only the shallow places. But others want to see where true grace lies. They are restless until we traverse there together."

Siddhārtha asked, "But we cannot be happy unless our hearts are happy, can we?"

"Yes, in many ways, it is easier for my followers to follow the law given to us by Moses. It is easy not to kill—see, I am not doing it now—but that does not mean I am truly following the law. If I have anger toward my sister or brother, it is as if I committed murder."

Siddhārtha thought for a bit and then responded, "That is a very difficult path indeed. How does one know another's intentions? I cannot look into your heart and gaze at your motivations."

"Certainly, you cannot. This is why the real law is one of love. It is harder to love one's neighbor than not to kill one's neighbor.

It is harder to care for another than to not steal from them. The harder path is the journey of loving one another and this world that has been bequeathed to us for our care. Again, it is to become love itself just as God is love."

"Then a person is happy when a person truly loves in this way?" Siddhārtha asked.

"That is where happiness begins and where it ends. When we open our hearts in love and receive the love that is given back, the result is happiness."

Siddhārtha added, "And sometimes it is not given back."

Yēšūa responded, "This can be happiness as well. It can be self-contained. We can freely love and not expect to have love come back to us."

Siddhārtha added, "This is because when we love without expectation, we have fulfilled the right action, the right intention, the right thoughts, right perspective, right speech, right mindfulness, right concentration, and right effort.

Like you said, it need not come back to us. It need not be about how others respond."

Yēšūa pondered a bit, "I like that. Sometimes our actions follow our thoughts, and sometimes we change what we believe because we acted differently. Sometimes our actions and thoughts are moved by our emotions. Sometimes our emotions can be shaped by what we do and how we think.

I often tell my people that their sins were forgiven. This was not because they did something wrong against me or against God, but because they believed that somehow, they were cursed for being poor, or being sick, or being childless. But to hear that there was no longer this judgment was a relief for many. They were free of these burdens and could be happy in whatever place they were in."

"This seemed as though the greatest miracle is to love some-one as they are," Siddhārtha replied.

A clowder of cats looked up at them. A few of the kittens walked up and rubbed themselves on Siddhārtha's ankle. Their purring tickled his leg, and he smiled in delight. Yēšūa squatted down to pet one behind its ears. It rattled its tiny head after Yēšūa stopped, a blur of motion.

Siddhārtha and Yēšūa walked up to a stream at the edge of the forest. The smooth rocks had been shaped by an eternity of polishing. The waters flowed from a source that seemed to have no beginning—and therefore no end. A deer bent its neck to drink from the stream, then lifted its gaze to look deeply into the two. They looked back into the ocean that was its spirit.

"Let me ask a personal question," Siddhārtha said in a tone unlike before.

"Please," urged Yēšūa.

"Were you happy doing what you were doing? Were you ful-filled?"

"Thank you, my friend. No one had ever asked me that. The truth was that there were many times that my heart broke over the injustices of my world and the people who suffered these in-justices. There were many days of tears.

But my fulfillment was not in the change I brought to this world, but in seeing people who saw and believed that the change was possible. They could look into themselves and see a whole world of possibility and promise. They were able to truly hear and see, or at least get a glimpse of how life could be different."

"And was it different for them? There are many Christians."

"Ha! Yes, there are many people who carry this name, but what does that mean? Do they possess a certain belief? Do they behave a certain way? Do they love others and have compassion for them?

Too often, people who deny happiness in themselves will want to deny happiness in another. They seek to be happy and don't get it, and therefore all will be miserable for their sake. Whether or not someone calls themselves a Christian or a Buddhist or an Atheist is unimportant to me. People will know they are my disciples simply because of their love.

May I ask the same about you? Were you truly happy in your life?"

Siddhārtha filled his mind with images of his wife and child, and all he had left behind to teach others about the Path.

Then he spoke.

"Even though I left my wife and son, Rāhula, on the day he was born. Ironically, his name means 'fetter' or 'bond' in our Sanskrit language. I thought he was to be a tether to my side.

But when he was released, he later returned to me and eventually became ordained as a priest. I lost nothing and gained everything. My happiness was in every moment—teaching those around me, meditating, tuning into a right way of life."

Like you, I wanted my disciples to bring compassion into the world with the right understanding of it.

In a way, I wanted to distill who we are down to the core—our suffering, our desires, our happiness. I found that this is what I needed, and then this was what I shared.

Could I have been happy as a wealthy prince? Perhaps.

But I would not have known how to relieve the suffering of others."

"Would that have denied who you truly are? You would not have known that also, correct?" Yēšūa questioned.

"Again, that is tricky because who of us knows who we are truly? This is the paradox of self. We seek to change ourselves. But if we do not know what we are, what is it we hope to change?

If we explore ourselves, are we not only chasing what we wish to leave behind?

Then all that remains is to become what we are not.

Who can grasp this?"

Yēšūa added, "Yes. I felt much the same way. I could have worked as a carpenter, as a day laborer like my father, and done well for myself in a trade. I could have had a wife and family.

But would I have known what was truly possible for me and others?"

"Would you have lived in regret for not fulfilling this call to be what you were meant to be?" Siddhārtha asked, perhaps an inquiry about his own life.

"I really don't know because I did not do otherwise. What I don't ever regret is loving all those whom I met, and doing it in the best way I knew how.

I concluded that we are complex beings, but love is simple. Love can be a thought, an action, and a feeling. But it is also more than those things. It is a position. A direction and a goal. It should guide us where we should go. If we open our hearts to its possibilities, no matter what the result, then we are on the right track."

Siddhārtha smiled and expressed, "I feel as though the world would be a better place if all people lived with this kind of heart, moved in the world with this kind of being."

"I feel the same way. If more people lived in harmony and peace with the world, then life would be better for everyone and all things. The Kingdom would truly be realized, and people would be aware that it is in their midst," Yēšūa returned.

Siddhārtha explained, "It seems for both of us, happiness is both easy and difficult to obtain."

Yēšūa asked, "How so?"

"While residing at the Jetavana Monastery in Savatthi, I came

JESUS AND BUDDHA TALK

to know a certain man in the community who was known for his happiness and contentment. One day, someone approached him and asked, 'What is the secret to your happiness?'

The man replied, 'There are four things that bring me happiness and contentment. First, I do not regret my past actions. I have lived my life in such a way that I can look back without remorse, knowing that I have done no wrong.'

Then he spoke of his lack of remorse. 'I do not feel remorse or guilt over my deeds. My actions have been upright, and my conscience is clear,' he shared.

Then, he told of contentment, 'I am satisfied with what I have. I do not crave for any more than what I have or feel dissatisfaction. My happiness comes from appreciating and being content with what I possess.'

And lastly, he spoke of how he shared everything, 'I am generous with my resources. I share what I have with others, and this act of giving brings me immense joy and satisfaction.'

To be like this man is to both let go of everything and to embrace it all.

Happiness is right there for us, within our grasp. But we must take it and let go of everything else. It is the 'everything else' that is difficult to release."

Yēšūa inquired, "But is this not life's course? We, as you said, cannot hold on to things forever. There must be a source of all happiness that can grow within us and sustain us."

"Happiness cannot be bound to the fleeting pleasures and circumstances of life. It cannot be one moment here, and the next moment gone. It cannot be about what happens to us because that is beyond our control and scope. We can only govern how we think, perceive, and respond to our world.

My bhikkhus, after I departed, became a refuge to themselves, an island to themselves. The Dhamma—my teachings—became their island, their refuge, their place of happiness."

Yēšūa commented, "It seems that those students learned to differentiate what we want and what we need."

Siddhārtha inquired, "How so?"

"They sought happiness not in what they could attain, but in what was given to them in their community. The food they ate, the place they slept, the friendships they shared—all of it came through their life together. This is what all of us truly need: to find the Kingdom in this way. Seek first this kinship, and everything else will find its way to you."

Siddhārtha commented, "Yes. Happiness will never come to those who fail to appreciate what they already have."

Yēšūa replied, "People are happy when they have reason to live. When there is meaning to their lives. People have visions for what they want their lives to be. Those who realize them are happy, but many hold on to it too tightly, knowing the tenuous nature of what they possess. They are often scared to lose it and would even take away another's happiness rather than lose what they have.

But take away the job, the spouse, the partner, the friend, and even health, and happiness slowly vanishes. Most do not have the patience and endurance of Job. When the world falls apart, many curse God and ask, 'Why me?' or 'What have I done to deserve any of this?'"

"Then how can they have meaningful lives, lives truly worth living?" Siddhārtha asked.

"It is well that people make plans, have goals, dream, and obtain fulfillment of them. It is well that they are happy in that way and can use their wealth to help their families and others. Those are noble desires. However, what is meaningful is not in what we do or possess, but in who we are."

"Is this a return to the notion of being we've been talking about?" Siddhārtha asked.

"The fullness of a person, the pinnacle of their existence, is in who they are, however they are, in whatever place they are.

The lilies of the field are happy because they are clothed in splendor that even King Solomon's riches could not surpass. The same is true for the birds of the air. They neither labor nor sow nor harvest, yet God provides for them abundantly. They are happy simply being what they are, never burdened by thoughts of what their lives mean."

Siddhārtha prompted, "Does this mean they no longer have any wants or needs?"

"No, I'm saying the opposite. One of my disciples, Peter, was a fisherman at the Lake of Galilee when I called him to use his skills to help others bring about the reality of the Kingdom. I could tell that, in his heart, he wanted more than just to catch fish—he wanted to become the person he was created to be.

But often we do not know who we are, and we seek countless distractions to satisfy the craving within us. This is especially dangerous if we catch even a glimpse of our true self — and yet spend our lives not living into that deeper sense of being.

After my death, Peter and the other disciples returned to their fishing nets. He was heartbroken and disappointed. He believed that this was all he could do."

"What happened to him?"

"He was distraught. He could not catch anything until I returned and showed him where to cast his nets. He could not retreat into his former life after he had experienced what he was meant to do.

It was there, on the shores of Galilee, that I asked him if he truly loved me — that if he did, he would take care of the people I had gathered, my sheep. I asked him three times so that he could feel, deep in his heart, that this was what he truly desired.

He had denied me three times, and he needed to know — to feel in every cell of his body — that love outweighed whatever wrong he had done."

"Remarkable! But it seems their happiness is not dependent on anything outside of their own existence," Siddhārtha reflected. "But isn't this being self-centered?"

"There is a difference between self-centeredness and being-centeredness. We cannot exist without one another."

Siddhārtha raised his index finger and said, "Yes, this is what one of my disciples described as 'inter-being.'"

"Please say more," Yēšūa eagerly prompted.

"All things are connected. When I see this blade of grass before us, or this cup, I should also see the clouds. The clouds bring rain, which nourishes the grass so it can grow.

The grass decays and returns to the soil. Water from the clouds mixes with the earth to form mud, and from the mud comes clay.

The cup is fired in an oven made of bricks, much like the clay from which the cup itself is formed.

The wood for the kiln comes from trees that depend on the soil and the rain.

Everything depends on everything else. Remove one thing, and the others cannot exist."

Siddhārtha thought of his own happiness and continued, "When I lived as a young prince, I was happy where I was. But the suffering of others — knowing about death and disease — changed my perspective of myself, and therefore, my meaning.

My happiness then became a need to remedy the problem of suffering and to teach others what I had learned.

Relieving suffering became, for me, a way to be happy. It expressed, as you say, my sense of being in this world.

It seems that as we make our way through life, 'who we are' is constantly challenged.

And so we must always return to that place and ask again: Who are we, really?

But it always comes back to this puzzling thing — what is the self?

What are we, but the attributes of any object? What are you but the color of your hair, the shape of your face, the size of your body, and all the parts that make you a person?

Take away each part, and what is left? This is what continues to puzzle me: what truly constitutes a self?"

Yēšūa commented, "Perhaps we need not be too philosophical. Is it not enough that you are here, delighting in the cup, the tea, and perhaps the conversation? And is it not in relation to these things that you are full in your being?

If you are a friend, then that is what you are right now. If you are a brother, then that is what you are right now. And so it is with everything. That is what brings us together.

I can be happy that I exist as me, and you exist as you, and we relate to each other as such."

"What if you did not have a partner, family, or companions? Then what are you? Can one still be happy without these relationships?" Siddhārtha challenged.

"We can be happy even then — when friends are gone, when family is gone. You are always related to another being in some way. You are always in relationship with something or someone. You can always be loved, and love another, and even become the very essence of love.

The possibility is always there. I am, therefore you are. You are, therefore I am. And that is who we are. That is the 'I am' of it all. That is where the Kingdom is, in you, and all around you.

Here is my point and I think where both our lives intertwine: when we truly can find and live into the core of our being, then that will give us the ability to love fully into all things. And this is the most important result of our existence.

Love makes all things possible. Love created the universe. Love keeps the stars and planets in motion. Love motivates all of us. Without it there would be simply impossibility. Nothingness."

"This is why each and every person, each and every thing, is important. But are you talking here about existence?" Siddhārtha asked, then added, "Can we simply be happy in our existence?"

Yēšūa explained, "If we ground our existence in an eternal relationship — a connection to the Divine ground of being — then we can be eternally happy."

As he spoke, he pressed one foot into the earth — not stomping, but planting his leg firmly into the ground.

"Please say more," Siddhārtha prompted.

"All of us stand on something. We exist in something, at least at the present moment. This existence is held together by something greater than ourselves, and perhaps that is why you doubt if we are anything without the qualities that make us who we are. Nevertheless, there is something that glues all those qualities together. It holds us and supports us.

I called it the 'Kingdom of God' because people at that time understood the context of those words to mean a domain, a reign, a place. However, it was unlike the Kingdom of other countries where control and conquest were what brought people together."

At that instance Yēšūa's mind flashed to all the people who suffered under the reign of the Roman Empire. The forced conquest of his native land could not be easily forgotten. This became

JESUS AND BUDDHA TALK

the context for his life's work, his ministry.

He continued, "I would often say, 'The Kingdom of God is like a treasure found in a field. When a man finds it, he sells everything he owns to buy that field.' When we find that which gives us true meaning — that which binds us to all things — it becomes our most valuable possession."

There is an eternal I AM, the source of all life. All beings thirst for this source, but humans, reaching for what is nearest, drink what cannot satisfy. This is the ground of which I am speaking."

Siddhārtha responded, "Yes, but existence is a fragile thing. All things move in and out of existence. Can happiness be anchored to such impermanence?"

"As you know, nothing is ever truly destroyed, only changed. Change is painful, but it is this pain that can propel us toward happiness. Pain tells us that something is wrong, or that something needs to be fixed, or tended to. When we remedy the hurt rightly — letting it be exposed to light and air — it begins to heal," Yēšūa explained.

They returned to the place where they had started and sat down once more.

Siddhārtha added, "People often say that all I teach is about suffering and the end of suffering. This might be an overstatement, but it is central to what we call the Dhamma. It is the path — the way — to extinguish our desires, even if only for a moment, so that we might find peace.

Desire is the flame, the suffering, that burns inside. It can consume us if we allow it to run amok. It is central because people often let their suffering spiral into thoughts and behaviors that cause even more suffering. It is a fire that can consume them entirely.

But for you, suffering is a way to recognize what is wrong."

Yēšūa affirmed, "It is not that I do not wish to end needless suffering. Of course, I do. It would be cruel not to. But I wish to allow suffering to tell us something — about our longing for life, for fulfillment, and for happiness."

Siddhārtha acknowledged, "That is quite true. Only when we acknowledge pain and suffering can we become aware of another way. Only when we stop resisting the truth about our lives are we free to see that we hold the key to freedom. It seems we are both prisoner and warden."

Yēšūa nodded and replied, "Perhaps we build our walls for safety at first — to shield ourselves from the storms of life. It is natural. It is human. But if we are not careful, the walls we build for protection can become the walls that imprison us."

Siddhārtha reflected, "Yes. Seeking safety is not wrong. It is a kindness we offer ourselves. But when safety becomes the only aim, we forget that life asks us to move, to grow, to step beyond the walls."

Yēšūa added, "The grace is that the door is never locked. The key is always within reach — even if we have forgotten where we placed it.

But for most people, sight and hearing are not restored overnight. It takes a lifetime of revelation and encounter. And still, few choose it. But when it is found, it becomes the easier path to take."

Siddhārtha tenderly responded, "Your patience seems eternal. I think it is because of your love for humanity."

Yēšūa replied, "I am bound to them, for I was born in their image. I have seen that your love is also great. Your hope is for all to find enlightenment, to see beyond themselves and their connection to the world."

"Thank you, my friend and brother, for this beautiful day to contemplate these truly sacred truths," Siddhārtha said.

"I am grateful as well for your heartfelt words. May we meet for many more conversations," Yēšūa acknowledged and slowly stood up.

Siddhārtha joined him. He brought the palms of his hands together, raised them to his chin, and bowed his head slightly. Yēšūa smiled, bowed, and wished him *shalom*.

The sun was setting over the hill, and the clouds filtered its rays into bright peach, orange, and crimson. The stars began to peek out from the violet sky. A horse neighed. An ox lowed. The waters still flowed through the banks of the river, as they have always done — now and forever.

POSTSCRIPT:
SEEING CLEARLY AND
FEELING DEEPLY

Jesus was told by his critics, "Physician, heal yourself." They recognized that he sought to bring wholeness to wounded people. The Buddha was a kind of physician in his own right, able to diagnose the problem of suffering as rooted in desire. One was about embodiment; the other, detachment.

But what if the way forward is not to pick one or the other, but to move forward with grace and balance? We can enter into the places of our deepest desires without being consumed by them. We can also seek not to be disturbed by the chaos of our environment without becoming unaware of those who are marginalized and suffering.

It takes finesse, but it can be done by embracing a view of human beings that reflects both our transitory nature and our great potential for transformation. In the West, our culture has an obsession with identity. But what if who we are is not as fixed as we think? Think about who we were when we were children. Are we the same persons? We say we are, but we only possess a simulacrum of our former selves. Physically, most of our exterior cells are replaced every seven years. The concept of identity—from the Latin word *idem*, meaning "same"—is a way to group people together by culture, nationality, ethnicity, and citizenship. We can easily see how identity becomes untethered when a person seeks to be different—yet they still appear the same as everyone else.

It is understandable to desire a fixed notion of identity, especially when, for many people, their identities have been either misconstrued or forced on them unwillingly. This is often a weak-minded attempt by a majority culture to place people into categories in order to better understand them. However, we also need to be careful not to fall into these same mistakes, lest they also imprison us.

Ironically, the more a person seeks to cling to their identity, the more they realize it is a fleeting concept. We only come to know who we are by abandoning fixed notions of who we are. We are not one thing, or even a sum of things. I am not only a U.S. citizen, or Vietnamese-American, or a man, or a writer, or an artist, or a husband, or whatever else I can add. I am something much more profound, connected to a larger reality. The problem in our society is the idea that if we only knew "who we are," we might resolve an ache within us. But no matter how important identity is, there is something deeper and greater waiting to emerge—to be enlightened, to be resurrected.

We experience the world, make sense of those experiences, and are also challenged by them. These challenges push us to change—sometimes in positive ways, sometimes in negative ones. We either become adaptive, or we retreat into protecting our sense of self—and in doing so, we deepen the suffering. But the ache is the calling.

What we see in these two spiritual masters is that, in dialogue, they give us a way to resolve something deeply human. Their journeys are both outward and inward, an exit and a return. Had they clung too tightly to who they thought they were—or to who others thought they were—their wisdom, knowledge, and experiences would have remained as static as those self-imposed notions. But they both realized they were much more.

We know the temporary nature of our existence all too well, yet we cannot avoid living in this embodied form. To deny our desires is to deny something essential about who we are. But to see desire as an end in itself is unsatisfying. Desire points us toward something greater—a truer calling that offers what we truly seek. Desire becomes the path by which we walk. Not alone.

For we have the wisdom and insight of these two—and many others—who continue to walk with us.

Jesus and Buddha Talk

Glossary of Terms

Anicca – The Pali term meaning impermanence.

Anatta – The Pali term meaning no-self, a lack of essence.

Beatitudes – A term referring to Jesus' statements of blessing at the beginning of his Sermon on the Mount (in the Gospel of Matthew) and Sermon on the Plain (in the Gospel of Luke). The word is derived from the Latin *beatus* meaning "blessed." It is paraphrased in the above text.

Ben adam (Hebrew) bar 'anash (Aramaic) – Termed used in Jewish apocalyptic literature, meaning "Son of Humanity."

Birds of the Air and Lilies of the Fields – Illustrations that are part of the Sermon on the Mount in Matthew 6:25-33

Bikkus – Buddha's disciples

Bodh Gaya – The place of Buddha's enlightenment

Bodhi Tree – The sacred fig tree under which Buddha had his enlightenment.

Buddha, the – A title meaning "The Awaken One," referring to the Buddha's enlightenment.

Christ, the – A Greek title meaning "The Anointed One." It is a translation of the Hebrew title, *Ha Mashiach* or the Messiah.

Deer Park – The deer sanctuary in Isipatana created by the lord of Vārānasī and is the site of the Siddhārtha Gautama's first sermon.

Devil, the – The personification of evil, developed during the Second Temple Period.

Dhamma – The teachings of the Buddha. The word is derived from the Sanskrit word dharma and often used interchangeably.

Dhammapada – A collection of the sayings of the Buddha. It is a compound word derived from dhamma meaning "doctrine" and meaning "foot." Portions are paraphrased in the above text.

Dharma – The Sanskrit term meaning duty

Eightfold Path (or the Noble Eightfold Path) – For Buddha, this is the way of enlightenment. From *Samyutta Nikaya* 45.8

Four Noble Truths (Dhammacakkappavattana Sutta) – Consists of four interrelated concepts: *dukkha* (suffering), *tahna* (desire), *nirodha* (the extinguishing of desire), and *marga* (the path of enlightenment). From the Samyutta *Nikaya* 56.11

Four Sights – What prince Siddhārtha saw that helped him on the path to enlightenment: the old man, the sick man, the dead man, and the ascetic

Happy Man, The Story of the (Sukha-vihara Sutta) – A story about how a man found the source of happiness and contentment. From the *Anguttara Nikaya* 3.36

Inner Being – A term used to describe what Buddhists emphasize as the inner life of the person

Interdependence – Also known as "dependent origination" or "dependent arising," this is the Buddhist concept that the underlying principle of reality is the interconnected. All things arise from other factors and causes. Vietnamese Zen Buddhist monk, Thích Nhất Hạnh further developed this notion in the term "Interbeing" from the French word *interêtre* and the Vietnamese words *tiếp hiện* (realizing being in touch with). Interbeing is often described in contrast to Western views of causality, where the cause precedes the effect in a linear fashion. Things "interbe" as they are both the cause and the effect of other things, and these other things are also the causes and effects of the prior things, no longer making them prior. Buddhists often illustrate this with the analogy of the two bundle of reeds. If standing, they lean on each other for support. If one falls, the other falls as well, thus illustrating the interconnection of all things.

Isipatana (Sarnath) – The place in northeast India where Siddhārtha Gautama delivered his first sermon. The name "Sarnath" means "Lord of the Deer." See Deer Park

Job – A character in the Hebrew Scriptures who undergoes testing from *ha satan* a title meaning the accuser. *Ha satan* acts as the prosecuting attorney in God's court to determine the righteousness of humans.

Judean Desert – The desert in the southern region of Israel and the place of Jesus' forty day fast and temptation by the devil

Karma – A Sanskrit word meaning the law of cause and effect

Kingdom of God (Kingdom of Heaven) – A termed used by Jesus to designate God's reign on earth. It is the kinship between God's people and the earth in relation to each other.

Kisa-Gotami, The Story of – A tale of a woman who experiences personal tragedy and learns about the universality of suffering comes from the *Majjhima Nikaya* 44

Māra – The personification of evil and the dark impulses of humanity. The name is derived from the Sanskrit word meaning "death" or "destruction."

Micah, the prophet – A prophet of the southern kingdom of Judah in the 8th century BCE, before the fall of Israel. The passage reference is from Micah 6:8 – "He has told you, O mortal, what is good, /and what does the Lord require of you / but to do justice and to love kindness / and to walk humbly with your God?" (NRSVUE).

Moksha – The Sanskrit word for liberation from *saṃsāra*

Nazareth – The town in North Israel where Jesus grew up and spent most of his time in ministry.

Nibbāna (Nirvāṇa, Sanskrit) – The Pali word meaning "to quench the thirst."

Pāli – The language used by Siddhārtha Gautama. It is described as a Middle Indo-Aryan language used in Buddhist liturgy.

Pipal tree – The sacred fig tree. See Bodhi Tree

Pharisees – A religious sect that formed during the Second Temple Judaism that held to the strict interpretation of the Law or Torah. Their name is from the Hebrew meaning "Separate Ones."

Poison Arrow – The metaphor of the poison arrow comes from Majjhima Nikaya 72 and it intended to get at the root cause of human suffering rather than spend time on metaphysical speculation.

Rich Young Ruler, The – A story found in Mark 10:17-27, about Jesus' interaction with a wealthy noble who realized he could not follow Jesus because of his possessions

Saṃsāra – The Sanskrit word for the cycle of birth, life, death, and rebirth. It tied to the idea that all things are reincarnated in a cyclical cosmology. The word has both the meaning of "world" and "wandering."

Sangha – The Buddhist monastic order or community composed of monks, nuns, and laypersons.

Second Temple Judaism – The Jewish religion as it developed during the Second Temple Period, which occurred after the rebuilding of the second Jerusalem Temple in 516 BCE and lasting until 70 CE when the Romans destroyed the Temple. During this time several Jewish sects emerged including the Essenes, Pharisees, Sadducees, and Zealots. See Pharisees

Shakya clan – A tribe existing in northeastern region of South Asia during the Iron Age. Buddha is sometimes called Buddha Shakyamuni

Shalom – The Hebrew word meaning "peace," often used as a greeting

Sin – The Hebrew and Greek concept of "missing the mark." In the Hebrew, the word *chata* (חָטָא). In Greek, *hamartia* (ἁμαρτία) means to not hit the mark or achieve a goal. is used as an archery term used to describe how a person misses the target. The idea developed from a secular concept into a moral and ethical concept to mean guilt, alienation, trespass, or failure. In Greek usage, sin also carries the weight of ignorance.

Sinned-against – A victim of sin, someone affected by the results of sin, whether personal, communal or systematic. The term is a translation of theologian, Andrew Sung Park, from the Korean notion of *han* or woundedness and expressed with biblical language.

Synagogue – The Jewish place of learning and worship developed during the Second Temple period by the Pharisaical sect of Judaism.

Tahna – The Pali word meaning "longing," "desire," or "thirst"

Three Poisons – Greed (or lust), hatred (or anger), and delusion (or ignorance)

Three Trainings – Virtue, mind, and wisdom. These are the three partitions of the Eightfold Path.

Jesus and Buddha Talk

maps

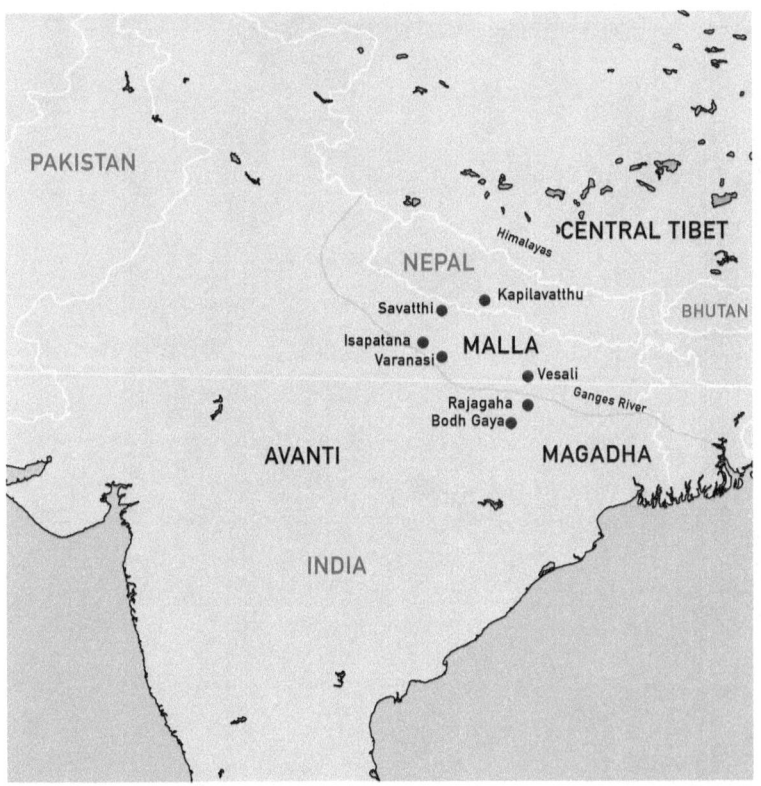

South Asia, 6th–5th Centuries BCE

JESUS AND BUDDHA TALK

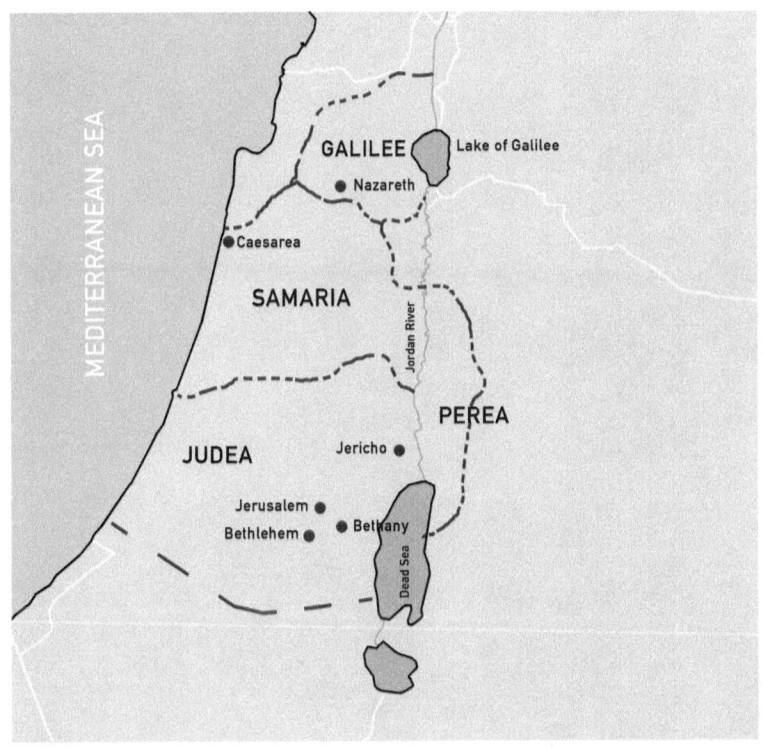

Palestine, First Century

JESUS AND BUDDHA TALK

ACKNOWLEDGEMENTS

When this book began, there was much desire and suffering, but not so much happiness. Another life transition brought many challenges, but like all crises, it also offered opportunities to explore meaning through some of the world's most important traditions. I am thankful that during this time, there were people who embodied what it means to live a happy life. They did not merely seek happiness—they sought to become it. To them, I am deeply grateful.

To Jamie Portwood, who read and reread, offering critiques, corrections, commentary, and many, many questions. To my Zen and the Art of Motorcycle Maintenance crew: Quique Autrey, Nate Dickerson, Aaron Inkrott, and John Norwood.

Special thanks to those who continue to be eternal supporters and patrons of my work, namely Mark Dostert and Kate Martin Williams. Your love for beautiful words and books brings everything important together.

Thank you to those whose holy presence reminds me that

there is more to life than the things we do: Rev. Julius Wardley, Rev. Patrick Miller, David (Doc) Brown and Trayce Wear, Mayrua and Franck Boursier, Laura and Travis Reed, Mary and Dick Steele.

To my book club: Pam and Rob, John Hays, Lisa, Frank, Allison, both the OG group and the new. Thank you to my Substack community, People of the Way. Your support has continued to allow me to follow wherever the pen and keyboard have taken me.

Roxy and Layla, our animal companions, are sources of strengh especially when I did not know I needed it. Paula Nguyễn Lưu, you have made my life more wonderful than I could ever have imagined.

ABOUT THE AUTHOR

Phuc Luu (福 刘) *immigrated* with his family to the United States from Vietnam when he was four. He is a theologian, philosopher, and artist based in Houston, Texas, whose work seeks to narrow the divide between ideas and beauty. If theology is the language we use to speak of God, Luu aims to give voice and grammar to what theology has not yet dared to say.

He served for seven years on the Nobel Peace Prize nominating committee for the American Friends Service Committee (Quakers) and holds degrees in theology (MDiv, PhD) and philosophy (MA). Yet he would say he has learned the most from the places where people ask difficult questions—where they live in the land between pain and hope, and where their stories are told.

His first book, *Jesus of the East: Reclaiming the Gospel for the Wounded* (Herald Press, 2020), explored how Jesus' work was to bring healing to the sinned-against. His forthcoming book, *In Their Image: How Atheists and Evangelicals Created the Same God*, challenges the false divide between belief and unbelief. It examines how both atheists and evangelicals have constructed visions of God that limit the depth of faith, doubt, and human experience. This book invites readers beyond binary thinking to uncover a more expansive and transformative understanding of the divine—one not rooted in certainty, but open to mystery and change.

Photograph by Paula Nguyen Luu